Fact Finders ™

Biographies
Marco
POLO

by Kathleen McFarren

Consultant:

John P. Boubel, Ph.D.
History Professor, Bethany Lutheran College
Mankato, Minnesota

Capstone
press

Mankato, Minnesota

Fact Finders is published by Capstone Press
151 Good Counsel Drive, P.O. Box 669, Mankato, Minnesota 56002
www.capstonepress.com

Library of Congress Cataloging-in-Publication Data
McFarren, Kathleen.
    Marco Polo / by Kathleen McFarren.
        p. cm.—(Fact finders. Biographies)
    Summary: An introduction to the life of the thirteenth-century Venetian explorer who
traveled along the Silk Road to the court of Kublai Khan in China.
    Includes bibliographical references and index.
    ISBN 0-7368-2490-1 (hardcover)
    1. Polo, Marco, 1254–1323?—Travel—Juvenile literature. 2. Explorers—Italy—
Biography—Juvenile literature. 3. Travel, Medieval—Juvenile literature. 4. Asia—
Description and travel—Juvenile literature. [1. Polo, Marco, 1254–1323? 2. Explorers.
3. Asia—Description and travel.] I. Title. II. Series.
G370.P9M44 2004
910.4—dc22   2003015361

Editorial Credits

Roberta Schmidt, editor; Juliette Peters, designer; Linda Clavel and Heather Kindseth,
    illustrators; Deirdre Barton and Kelly Garvin, photo researchers; Eric Kudalis,
    product planning editor

Photo Credits

Art Resource/Snark, 22
Corbis/Alison Wright, 16; Archivo Iconografico, S.A., 20; Robert Holmes, 6–7;
    Steve Bein, 17
Courtesy of MoneyMuseum, 21
Getty Images/Hulton Archive, 1, 10, 12–13, 23, 25
Index Stock Imagery/Ewing Galloway, 4–5
North Wind Picture Archives, cover, 9, 14–15
Stock Montage Inc., 11, 18–19

1 2 3 4 5 6 09 08 07 06 05 04

Table of Contents

Marco Polo

Two older men and one young man stepped into a huge tent of **silk** and bamboo. A 60-year-old man sat in front of them. He had dark hair and dark eyes. He was the great Kublai Khan.

The young man watched the two older men bow before Kublai Khan. They gave him gifts. They spoke to him in a strange language.

Kublai Khan welcomed the older travelers. He then asked about the young man. One of the older men answered. He said the young man was his son and Kublai Khan's servant.

The young man's name was Marco Polo. The year was 1275.

Marco Polo met Kublai Khan at Kublai Khan's home in Shang-tu.

Marco Polo served Kublai Khan in Asia for the next 17 years. Polo saw parts of the world that Europeans had never seen. A book was later written about his travels. His stories made many people want to **explore** new lands.

Chapter 2

A Beginning in Venice

Marco Polo was born in 1254. He grew up in Venice. Venice was one of the largest and richest cities in Europe at that time. Goods from all over the world went through Venice. Later, Venice became part of Italy.

The Polos sold and traded goods. They traveled often. When Marco Polo was a baby, his father, Niccolò, and uncle Maffeo Polo left Venice to trade goods in other countries. They were gone for 14 years. During that time, Marco Polo's mother died. Polo was raised by his aunt and other relatives.

Marco Polo possibly was born in this house on the island of Korcula in the Mediterranean Sea.

Marco Polo was 15 years old when his father and uncle returned to Venice. They told him stories about wonderful things they had seen in Asia.

Chapter 3

The Mysterious Land of Asia

By the 1200s, Europeans had traded with Asians for more than 1,000 years. Still, Europeans knew little about Asia. They only knew that Asia had silk and **spices** not found in Europe.

Goods between Europe and Asia were carried on the Silk Road. This series of trails stretched 5,000 miles (8,000 kilometers) between Europe and Asia. The people who lived between Europe and Asia controlled the trade.

Niccolò and Maffeo Polo were some of the first Europeans to visit central and eastern Asia. They traded goods there. They also met the ruler of the Mongol **Empire**.

Trade with Asia was very important to Europeans during the Middle Ages (400–1400).

▲ Kublai Khan was the ruler of the Mongol Empire from 1264 until 1294.

F A C T !

Mongol soldiers often ate dried yak or horse milk. If a soldier had no milk, he cut open a vein on his horse and drank the blood.

The Mongol Empire and Kublai Khan

In the early 1200s, a group of people called the Mongols **conquered** most of Asia. The Mongol Empire spread across land that is now Russia, China, Poland, and Hungary. Genghis Khan was the first ruler of this empire. In 1264, Genghis Khan's grandson Kublai Khan became ruler.

Kublai Khan was called the Great Lord of all the Khans. He wanted to know about the lands and people he ruled. He also wanted to learn about people from other lands.

Kublai Khan and the Polo Brothers

Kublai Khan was happy to meet Niccolò and Maffeo Polo. He had never met any people from Europe. He asked them about their land and rulers. He also was interested in their religion. Like most Europeans at that time, the Polos were **Christians**.

▼ Niccolò and Maffeo Polo met Kublai Khan in 1265.

In 1266, Kublai Khan sent the Polo brothers back to Europe. He asked them to bring him 100 men from their church to teach him about their religion. He also asked for some holy oil from Jerusalem. Many Christians believed this oil had healing powers.

It took the brothers three years to get home. By 1271, they were ready to return to Kublai Khan. They took 17-year-old Marco Polo with them.

The Polos traveled in a group called a caravan.
➡

aquesta carauana es partida delimpi
de sarrapamar adantayo :—

Chapter 4

The Journey

In the summer of 1271, the Polos set sail from Venice. They sailed south to Jerusalem. There, they got the holy oil for Kublai Khan. But they were not able to get 100 men from the church.

From Jerusalem, the Polos sailed north to Ayas. This city is in what is now Turkey. At Ayas, they began their long journey over land.

The Polos traveled through Asia Minor and Persia. Today these lands are known as Turkey, Iraq, and Iran. The Polos planned to sail from Hormuz on the Persian Gulf to China. But at Hormuz, they saw the ships were not strong enough. The Polos turned north and continued their journey over land.

This image of the Polos leaving Venice comes from a copy of Marco Polo's book about his travels.

▲ The Polos traveled through the Pamirs.

The Polos passed through the land that is now Afghanistan. They crossed hot deserts. They climbed high mountains. They then reached the farmlands of Kashgar. The farmlands were on the edge of Cathay, the area that is now China. The Polos knew they soon would cross the Gobi Desert.

The Gobi Desert was a dangerous place. It took at least 30 days to cross the desert. The Polos had heard that the blowing sands made strange noises. Some travelers said they heard voices and music. Travelers who followed the noises often got lost and died.

The Polos crossed the Gobi Desert safely. Kublai Khan heard about them and sent men to greet them. These men led the Polos to Kublai Khan's **palace** in Shang-tu.

The Polos reached Shang-tu in May 1275. Their journey had taken almost four years.

▲ The Polos had to cross the Gobi Desert to reach Kublai Khan.

F A C T !

On the journey, Marco Polo saw many things he had never seen before. In Asia Minor, he saw oil gushing from the ground. In Persia, he saw humped oxen called zebu.

Chapter 5

In Service to the Khan

Kublai Khan made the Polos his special guests. He was glad to see Niccolò and Maffeo Polo again. He thanked them for the holy oil. He also welcomed Marco Polo. During the following months, Kublai Khan gave special dinners and parties for the Polos.

When the summer ended, the Polos went with Kublai Khan to his winter palace in Khanbalik. This city is now part of Beijing, China. Marco Polo was amazed by this palace. The walls were covered with gold and silver. The roof was yellow, blue, green, and many other colors. Next to the palace were gardens, trees, and a lake.

Kublai Khan had a great palace in Khanbalik, where the city of Beijing now stands.

Exploring Asia

Over the years, Kublai Khan sent Marco Polo on trips around the Mongol Empire. The great ruler wanted to know more about the land and people.

Marco Polo traveled throughout southeastern Asia. He saw that some lands were poor. Other lands were rich with silks, spices, and jewels.

Marco Polo met people who mined red and blue rubies.

Marco Polo saw many things that were different from Europe. In Europe, money was in coins. In Asia, the people used paper money. People in Europe did not take baths very often. People in Asia kept themselves very clean.

While Marco Polo traveled, Niccolò and Maffeo Polo stayed at the palace. They traded and became very rich.

The Polos stayed in Asia for 17 years. Kublai Khan did not want them to leave.

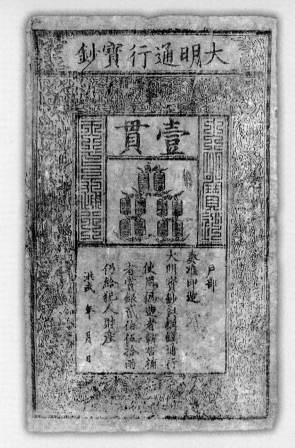

▲ The paper money that Marco Polo saw may have looked like this Chinese money from the Ming Dynasty (1368–1644).

FACT!

Marco Polo traveled from Siberia to India and from Korea to Armenia.

▲ The Polos sailed from China to Hormuz. They then left their ships and finished their journey by land.

Leaving Asia

The Polos finally found a way to go home. The ruler of Persia asked Kublai Khan for a wife. Kublai Khan chose his niece, Cocachin. Someone needed to take her to Persia. The Polos asked Kublai Khan if they could take Cocachin to Persia. Kublai Khan agreed.

The Polos sailed from China around 1292. They traveled on 13 ships with 600 people. Bad weather and sicknesses made the trip slow and hard. Only the Polos, Cocachin, and 14 other people survived the journey. After the Polos took Cocachin to Persia, they went home to Venice.

Home

The Polos reached Venice in 1295. Marco Polo had been only 17 years old when they left home. He returned as a 41-year-old man.

The people of Venice did not give Niccolò, Maffeo, and Marco Polo a warm welcome. No one could believe that the three travelers were the Polos. Their family had not heard from them in 24 years.

The Polos invited many people to a special dinner. After the meal, they cut open their old clothes. Jewels from Asia fell out. The people then believed that the three men were the Polos.

▲ When the Polos arrived at their home in Venice, their relatives would not let them in.

FACT!

Kublai Khan died in 1294 while the Polos were on their way home to Venice.

23

Chapter 6

Final Years

In the late 1290s, the city of Venice fought a war with the city of Genoa. Marco Polo was caught by soldiers from Genoa and put in jail. While there, he told another **prisoner** about his travels. This prisoner was a writer named Rustichello. Rustichello wrote a book about Marco Polo's travels. The book was called *Description of the World*. Today, the book is often called *The Travels of Marco Polo*.

Marco Polo went back to Venice after the war ended. He continued to trade and sell goods. He married Donata Badoer and had three daughters. Marco Polo died on January 8, 1324.

Yͤ Book of Ser Marco Polo yͤ Venetian concerning yͤ kingdoms of yͤ East:

Newly done into English.

by HENRY YULE c.b.

Second VOL.

Edition. IIᴰ

cité Quinsaí trente dou Grāi Caan
5 miglion et 6 cens mille
5 miglior et 7 cēs mille

Messer Marco Millioni telleth his story to Rustician of Pisa in the Prison at Genoa. ANNO D...

LONDON: JOHN MURRAY:

1874.

This 1874 cover of *Description of the World* shows Rustichello writing down the stories that Marco Polo tells him.

Lasting Impact

The story of Marco Polo and his adventures was popular for hundreds of years. *Description of the World* was copied into many languages. Some people believed the stories. Many other people thought Marco Polo lied about his travels.

Marco Polo was not the first European to reach Asia. But he was the first visitor to put his adventures in a book. His book helped people learn about the land and people in Asia. It made many people interested in exploring the world.

FACT!

Christopher Columbus read Marco Polo's book. Columbus wanted to reach the lands that Marco Polo had seen. He took a copy of the book with him when he crossed the Atlantic Ocean in 1492. But Columbus never reached Asia. He found the Americas instead.

The Travels of Marco Polo, 1271–1295

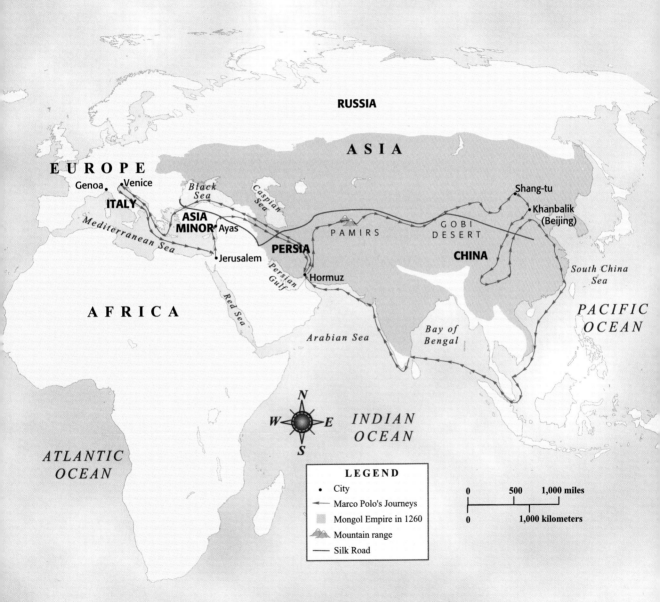

RUSSIA

ASIA

EUROPE

Genoa • • Venice

ITALY

Black Sea

Caspian Sea

Shang-tu

• Khanbalik
(Beijing)

ASIA
MINOR • Ayas

PAMIRS

GOBI
DESERT

Mediterranean Sea

PERSIA

• Jerusalem

Persian Gulf

• Hormuz

CHINA

South China Sea

AFRICA

Red Sea

Arabian Sea

Bay of Bengal

PACIFIC OCEAN

N
W E
S

INDIAN OCEAN

ATLANTIC OCEAN

LEGEND
- • City
- ← Marco Polo's Journeys
- ▒ Mongol Empire in 1260
- ▲ Mountain range
- — Silk Road

0   500   1,000 miles

0   1,000 kilometers

Fast Facts

- Marco Polo grew up in Venice.

- Marco Polo's father, Niccolò, and uncle Maffeo were traders. They were some of the first Europeans to visit Asia.

- Marco Polo traveled to Asia with his father and uncle.

- Kublai Khan ruled much of Asia from 1264 until 1294.

- Marco Polo served Kublai Khan for 17 years.

- When the Polos returned from Asia in 1295, they had been gone for 24 years. Their family did not recognize them.

- While Marco Polo was in jail, he told a prisoner named Rustichello about his travels. Rustichello wrote a book about some of Marco Polo's adventures. The book was called *Description of the World*.

Time Line

Life Events of Marco Polo

Marco Polo is born in Venice.

Polo meets Kublai Khan at Shang-tu.

Polo explores the Mongol Empire for Kublai Khan.

Polo returns to Venice.

Polo dies January 8.

1254 1264 1275 1275–1292 1294 1295 1324 1492

World Events

Kublai Khan becomes ruler of the Mongol Empire.

Kublai Khan dies.

Christopher Columbus crosses the Atlantic Ocean.

Glossary

Christians (KRISS-chuns)—people who believe in the religion of Christianity; Christianity is based on the life and teachings of Jesus Christ.

conquer (KONG-kur)—to defeat and take control of an enemy

empire (EM-pire)—a large territory ruled by a powerful leader

explore (ek-SPLOR)—to travel to find out what a place is like

palace (PAL-iss)—a large, grand home for a king, queen, or other ruler

prisoner (PRIZ-uhn-ur)—a person who is held by force

silk (SILK)—a soft, shiny material made from fibers produced by a silkworm; silk is often made into clothing.

spice (SPISSE)—something used to flavor foods

Internet Sites

FactHound offers a safe, fun way to find Internet sites related to this book. All of the sites on FactHound have been researched by our staff.

Here's how:
1. Visit *www.facthound.com*
2. Type in this special code **0736824901** for age-appropriate sites. Or enter a search word related to this book for a more general search.
3. Click on the **Fetch It** button.

FactHound will fetch the best sites for you!

Read More

Burgan, Michael. *Marco Polo: Marco Polo and the Silk Road to China.* Exploring the World. Minneapolis: Compass Point Books, 2002.

Herbert, Janis. *Marco Polo for Kids: His Marvelous Journey to China: 21 Activities.* Chicago: Chicago Review Press, 2001.

Strathloch, Robert. *Marco Polo.* Historical Biographies. Chicago: Heinemann Library, 2002.

Index